NOBLE HEARTS

NOBLE HEARTS

INSPIRING STORIES FOR MUSLIM BOYS

THE YOUNG & THE FAITHFUL

YUSUF ALIM

NESS HOUSE PRESS

To every young boy who dreams big and leads with his heart. And to the parents, teachers, and mentors who nurture these noble hearts, showing them how to shine their light in the world.

CONTENTS

INTRODUCTION

Dear Young Reader,

Welcome to "Noble Hearts," a collection of stories about boys just like you – boys who are discovering what it means to be a young Muslim in today's world. In these pages, you'll meet Ahmad, who learns about the power of prayer; Karim, whose generosity touches his whole neighborhood; and Omar, who turns into quite the Ramadan detective!

These stories are more than just adventures – they're windows into the beautiful teachings of Islam and how you can live them every day. Whether you're learning about caring for the Earth like Ibrahim, or helping spot the Eid moon with Zayn, you'll find that being a Muslim boy is about having a noble heart that's full of courage, kindness, and wisdom.

Each story comes with its own "Islamic Knowledge Corner" where you can learn more about our faith and how it guides us to be our best selves. As you read, you might recognize situations from your own life, and hopefully, these stories will help you navigate them with confidence and faith.

Remember, you have the potential to make a difference in the world, just like the boys in these stories. So come along on this journey, and let's explore together what it means to have a truly noble heart.

With hope and faith,

Yusuf

THE PRAYER THAT MOVES
MOUNTAINS

Ahmad stared at his bedroom ceiling, his alarm clock blinking 5:30 AM. The call to Fajr prayer echoed softly through his window from the nearby mosque. He pulled his blanket tighter, fighting the urge to go back to sleep.

"Just five more minutes," he whispered to himself, but then remembered his father's words from the night before.

"Ahmad, prayer isn't just about going through the motions. It's about building a connection with Allah. And like any connection, it needs dedication."

With a deep breath, Ahmad pushed aside his warm blanket and headed to make wudu. The cool water helped clear his sleepy mind as he quickly performed his ablution so that he could quickly say his prayers... and quickly get back to bed.

In two weeks, Ahmad would be competing in his school's annual Science Olympiad. He had been chosen to represent his class, and the thought made his stomach flutter with nerves. The competition seemed like a mountain too high to climb, especially since Zain, last year's winner – and two whole years older than Ahmad – was competing again. Zain always seemed to know everything about science, and he was known for winning science competitions around the state.

Zain wasn't the only good competitor at this year's Science Olympiad. Ahmad worried he'd come last and embarrass himself. All the other competitors seemed so intimidating.

As Ahmad laid out his prayer mat facing the qibla, he remembered what his Islamic studies teacher, Ustadh Kareem, often said: "Prayer gives you strength. It's not just about fulfilling an obligation – it's about finding peace and guidance in every challenge."

The morning prayer felt different this time. Instead of rushing through the movements, Ahmad focused on each word, each rakah. When he finished, he remained seated on his prayer mat, raising his hands in dua.

"Ya Allah, please help me prepare for this competition. Give me strength and wisdom."

Over the next two weeks, Ahmad noticed something changing. By waking up for Fajr prayer consistently, his days felt more organized. He found himself more focused during study sessions. Even his mother noticed the difference.

"MashaAllah, Ahmad," she smiled one evening as she found him reviewing his science notes after Maghrib prayer. "You're becoming so responsible."

During these two weeks, Ahmad also started spending time at the library during lunch breaks instead of playing football. His friend Yusuf, noticing this change, asked him why he was studying so hard.

"I want to do my best," Ahmad explained. "Not just to win, but because Allah teaches us to strive for excellence in everything we do. My father told me about the hadith where the Prophet Muhammad (peace be upon him) said that Allah loves when a person does something, they do it with perfection."

The morning of the competition arrived. As Ahmad walked into the school hall, he felt the familiar flutter of nerves. But this time, something was different. He had just prayed Fajr with his father at the mosque, and a sense of calm wrapped around him like a warm blanket.

The questions were challenging, just as he expected. But before answering each one, Ahmad took a deep breath and silently said "Bismillah," just as he did before starting each prayer. When he wasn't sure of an answer, he remembered the patience he had learned from his early morning prayers.

The competition was tight. Zain breezed through the questions with confidence, but Ahmad stayed focused, remembering all his preparation. In the final round, when asked about the phases of the moon – something Ahmad had learned while studying Islamic months and the lunar calendar with his father – he felt especially grateful for his faith's connection to science.

When the results were announced, Ahmad couldn't believe his ears. He had won second place, just behind Zain! But instead of feeling disappointed about not winning first place, Ahmad felt proud. He knew he had done his absolute best, and more importantly, he had learned something far more valuable than just science facts.

His classmates congratulated him, and even Zain came over to shake his hand. "That was really close,"

Zain said with a smile. "Your answer about the moon phases was brilliant!"

That evening, after Isha prayer, Ahmad's father found him sitting on his prayer mat.

"Baba," Ahmad said thoughtfully, "I used to think prayer was just something we had to do. But now I understand – it really does give us strength."

His father smiled, placing a gentle hand on Ahmad's shoulder. "Allah says in the Quran that we should seek help through patience and prayer. You've discovered this truth for yourself, my son. And remember, success isn't always about coming in first – it's about doing your best and growing closer to Allah in the process."

Ahmad nodded, looking at his Science Olympiad medal hanging on the wall. The mountain he had thought impossible to climb had been conquered, not just through studying, but through the strength he found in prayer. He had learned that sometimes the real victory isn't in the competition itself, but in the journey of self-improvement and growing closer to Allah.

That night, as the call to Fajr prayer woke him the next morning, Ahmad didn't hesitate. He knew that beyond the sleepiness and comfort of his warm bed, something more valuable awaited – a daily reminder that with faith, dedication, and prayer, any mountain could be moved.

Islamic Knowledge Corner

Did you know? Fajr is the first prayer of the day in Islam. It is performed at dawn, before sunrise, and consists of two rakah (units of prayer). The Prophet Muhammad (peace be upon him) said that the two rakah of Fajr are better than this world and everything in it. This early morning prayer teaches Muslims discipline, dedication, and the importance of starting each day remembering Allah.

The time for Fajr prayer begins at dawn (when the first light appears in the sky) and ends just before sunrise. This beautiful time of day is mentioned in the Quran: "Establish prayer at the decline of the sun until the darkness of the night and the Quran of dawn. Indeed, the recitation of dawn is ever witnessed." (17:78)

KARIM'S KIND HEART

Karim stood at his bedroom window, watching raindrops race down the glass. His piggy bank – or as he preferred to call it, his "charity box" – sat heavy in his hands. For three months, he had been saving his pocket money for a new bicycle. But something his grandmother had said during her visit last week kept echoing in his mind.

"Allah multiplies every act of charity, my dear grandson. When you give with a pure heart, you receive so much more in return."

The rain was falling harder now, and through the gray sheets of water, he could see Mr. Wilson, their elderly neighbor, struggling with his groceries. The old man's umbrella had turned inside out, and his paper bags were starting to tear.

Without hesitation, Karim grabbed his raincoat. "Mama!" he called out, rushing downstairs. "Can I go help Mr. Wilson?"

His mother looked up from her computer where she had been working. "MashaAllah, habibi. Take the big umbrella from the closet."

Splashing through puddles, Karim ran to his neighbor's aid. Mr. Wilson's face lit up at the sight of him. Together, they managed to save the groceries just before the bags completely gave way.

"Thank you, young man," Mr. Wilson said, catching his breath in his kitchen. "These old hands aren't as strong as they used to be."

Looking around, Karim noticed how empty Mr. Wilson's kitchen seemed. The calendar on the wall showed no marks or appointments, unlike the busy one in Karim's house. Something tugged at his heart.

That evening, during dinner, Karim was quieter than usual. His younger sister Sarah noticed first. "Are you sick?" she asked, poking his arm with her fork.

"I'm just thinking," Karim replied, pushing his rice around his plate. "Mama, Baba, can I use my bicycle money for something else?"

His parents exchanged glances. They knew how much Karim had wanted that bicycle. "What do you have in mind?" his father asked.

"I want to help Mr. Wilson. Today when I was at his house, I noticed he doesn't have much food in his kitchen. And he's always alone." Karim took a deep breath. "Maybe we could invite him for dinner sometimes? And maybe I could use some of my money to buy him groceries?"

His father put down his spoon, eyes shining with pride. "The Prophet Muhammad, peace be upon him, always encouraged us to care for our neighbors. This is a wonderful idea, son."

The next day after school, Karim and his mother went shopping. They bought fresh fruits, vegetables, and other essentials. While they were checking out, Karim spotted a small plant in a blue pot.

"Can we get that too?" he asked. "His kitchen window looks empty."

That afternoon, they delivered the groceries to a surprised and touched Mr. Wilson. But Karim didn't stop there. Each day after finishing his homework, he would spend some time with his elderly neighbor. Sometimes they would play chess, other times Mr. Wilson would tell stories about his younger days as a teacher.

Word of Karim's kindness spread through the neighborhood. Mrs. Ahmed from across the street started sending over her famous biryani every Thursday. The twins from two houses down began helping Mr. Wilson with his garden. Soon, the empty kitchen calendar was filled with dinner invitations and tea dates.

One Saturday morning, Karim was helping Mr. Wilson water his now-flourishing windowsill plants when they heard a commotion outside. Looking out, they saw several of their neighbors in the driveway, gathered around something.

"Karim! Come out!" Sarah was jumping up and down with excitement.

When Karim stepped outside, his jaw dropped. There stood a beautiful blue bicycle with a big bow on it. His father emerged from the group, grinning.

"The neighbors all pitched in," he explained. "Mrs. Ahmed, the Patels, the Clarks – everyone wanted to thank you for reminding us what it means to be a community."

Mr. Wilson placed a shaky hand on Karim's shoulder. "You gave up your bicycle money to help an old man. You didn't just bring groceries to my house, son. You brought life back to it."

Karim felt tears welling up in his eyes. He remembered his grandmother's words about charity being multiplied, but this was more than just getting back what he had given up. His small act of kindness had created a ripple effect, transforming their entire neighborhood into a closer, more caring community.

That evening, as Karim's family hosted a neighborhood dinner in their backyard, he looked around at all the smiling faces. Mr. Wilson was teaching Sarah how to play chess. Mrs. Ahmed was sharing her biryani recipe with Mrs. Patel. The twins were helping Karim's mother set up the dessert table.

His father sat down beside him. "You know, Karim, there's a beautiful hadith where the Prophet Muhammad, peace be upon him, said that charity never decreases wealth. Today, you've shown us all how true that is. Your kindness didn't just help one person – it helped our whole community grow richer in friendship and care."

Karim smiled, thinking about how one small decision on a rainy day had led to all of this. His grandmother was right – when you give with a pure heart, Allah truly multiplies your charity in ways you could never imagine.

As the evening wound down, Karim led everyone

in a heartfelt dua, thanking Allah for the blessing of neighbors and the opportunity to help others. His new bicycle gleamed in the setting sun, a reminder that the greatest rewards often come when we think of others before ourselves.

📚 *Islamic Knowledge Corner*

Did you know? Sadaqah (voluntary charity) is a fundamental aspect of Islam that goes beyond just giving money. The Prophet Muhammad (peace be upon him) said: "Every act of kindness is charity." This includes:

- Smiling at someone
- Helping someone with a heavy load
- Removing harmful things from the road
- Speaking kind words
- Even planting a tree is considered sadaqah

The Quran mentions that those who give charity will be rewarded abundantly: "The example of those who spend their wealth in the way of Allah is like a seed which grows seven spikes; in each spike is a hundred grains. And Allah multiplies [His reward] for whom He wills." (2:261)

Caring for neighbors holds a special place in

Islam. The Prophet Muhammad (peace be upon him) emphasized this so much that his companions thought neighbors might be included in inheritance rights. This teaches us the importance of building strong, caring communities.

THE RAMADAN DETECTIVE

Omar's stomach growled so loudly during science class that even his teacher, Mrs. Parker, paused mid-sentence. His best friend Ibrahim tried not to laugh but ended up snorting instead, which made the whole class burst into giggles.

"Sorry," Omar mumbled, his face turning red. "I'm fasting."

"Ah yes, Ramadan," Mrs. Parker smiled knowingly. She had learned a lot about the holy month since Ahmad won second place in the Science Olympiad last term. "Only three more hours until iftar!"

The mention of iftar only made Omar's stomach

protest louder. This was his first year fasting for the full month of Ramadan, and while he was proud of keeping all his fasts so far, his tummy hadn't quite gotten the memo about being patient.

As they left class, Ibrahim patted his back. "Don't worry. My first year fasting, my stomach growled so loud during a quiz that Karim – you know, the kind one that's really good at chess? – he thought there was a lion in the classroom!"

But Omar had bigger things on his mind than his noisy stomach. Something strange was happening at the mosque. The beautiful wooden donation box that had stood by the entrance for decades had disappeared three days ago. Uncle Hassan, the mosque's caretaker, was beside himself with worry. The box contained the community's donations for the annual Eid celebration and gifts for children in need.

"I'm going to solve this mystery before Eid," Omar declared to Ibrahim as they walked home. "And I think I know just how to do it!"

"Oh no," Ibrahim groaned. "Last time you said that, we ended up stuck in Mr. Lee's apple tree trying to rescue a cat that turned out to be a plastic bag."

"That was different!" Omar protested. "Besides,

detective work should be easier while fasting. You know, clearer mind and all that."

Ibrahim raised an eyebrow. "Is that why you put salt in your cereal during this morning's suhoor instead of sugar?"

"That was... a deliberate experiment in flavor combinations," Omar said with dignity, making Ibrahim double over with laughter.

Over the next few days, Omar started his investigation. He created a special "Detective's Journal" where he wrote down everything he noticed during taraweeh prayers. His younger sister Amira kept trying to peek at his notes, convinced he was writing down the location of his secret candy stash.

"I'm not hiding any candy!" he told her for the hundredth time.

"That's exactly what someone hiding candy would say," she replied wisely, before skipping off to join her friends.

Omar noticed something interesting during his observations. Every night after taraweeh prayers, he saw Mr. Wilson (Karim's elderly neighbor who had become a regular at the mosque's community iftars) talking intently with Uncle Hassan. They would look at papers together and then hurry off to the mosque's storage room.

"Suspicious," Omar muttered, writing in his journal with the special "detective pen" his mother had given him to keep him quiet during last year's Eid khutbah.

One evening, while helping set up for iftar in the mosque's courtyard with Ibrahim, Omar overheard Mr. Wilson say something about "the old box" and "tomorrow night." This was it – his chance to crack the case!

The next night, Omar convinced Ibrahim to stay back after prayers to investigate. They hid behind the large potted plants in the courtyard (the same ones Mrs. Ahmed always said needed more water, but everyone was too scared of her biryani-wielding authority to disagree).

"I can't believe I let you talk me into this," Ibrahim whispered. "We're going to get in so much trouble. And I'm missing my mom's special Ramadan kunafa!"

"Shhh!" Omar hissed. "Look!"

Mr. Wilson and Uncle Hassan were walking toward the storage room. The boys tiptoed after them, trying to be quiet – which wasn't easy because Omar had forgotten he was wearing his light-up sneakers that made space noises with each step.

Beep-whoosh. Beep-whoosh.

"Omar!" Ibrahim face-palmed.

Just as they reached the storage room door, Omar's shoes let out their loudest space-blast yet, and he tripped over his own feet, crashing right into Ibrahim. They tumbled through the door in a tangle of arms and legs – right at the feet of Uncle Hassan and Mr. Wilson.

"Well," said Uncle Hassan, looking down at them with twinkling eyes. "It seems our little detective has finally caught us."

Omar and Ibrahim looked up to see not only Uncle Hassan and Mr. Wilson but also several other community members, including Omar's parents. And there, in the middle of the room, stood the most beautiful wooden donation box they had ever seen – clearly new, but carved to look like the old one.

"The old box was falling apart," Uncle Hassan explained, helping the boys up. "Mr. Wilson here used to be a carpenter before he retired. When he saw how worried we were about the old box, he offered to make us a new one as a gift to the mosque."

"We wanted to keep it a surprise for Eid," Mr. Wilson added. "Something special for the community that had welcomed me so warmly, thanks to your friend Karim's kindness earlier this year."

Omar's face broke into a huge grin. "So there was no theft! Just a secret Ramadan surprise!"

"Indeed," his father laughed. "Though perhaps not so secret, thanks to some very enthusiastic detective work and some very noisy sneakers."

Everyone burst out laughing, and Omar's shoes chose that exact moment to let out another cheerful *beep-whoosh*, making them laugh even harder.

Later that night, as they enjoyed Mrs. Ibrahim's kunafa (she had saved them each a piece), Omar looked at his friend. "You know what? Maybe I'm not cut out to be a detective."

"What gave it away?" Ibrahim grinned. "The space shoes, the salt cereal, or the plastic bag cat?"

"Very funny," Omar rolled his eyes. "But you know what I learned? Sometimes what looks like a mystery is just people doing good deeds in secret. Like Mr. Wilson and his beautiful gift."

"That's very wise of you, Omar," came a voice behind them. It was Ahmad, who had started volunteering at the mosque during Ramadan. "The Prophet Muhammad, peace be upon him, said that amongst the seven types of people who will be shaded by Allah on the Day of Judgment is the person who gives charity so secretly that their left hand doesn't know what their right hand has given."

Omar nodded thoughtfully, then brightened. "Hey, does this mean I can stop writing in my Detective's Journal?"

"Absolutely not!" Amira appeared out of nowhere. "I still need to find that candy stash!"

📚 *Islamic Knowledge Corner*

Did you know? The act of giving charity secretly is highly praised in Islam. The Quran mentions: "If you disclose your charitable expenditures, they are good; but if you conceal them and give them to the poor, it is better for you." (2:271)

Ramadan is a special time for giving charity. The Prophet Muhammad (peace be upon him) was already the most generous of people, but he was even more generous during Ramadan. This teaches us that while fasting helps us understand the hunger of others, it should also inspire us to be more charitable.

During Ramadan, Muslims fast from dawn (Fajr) until sunset (Maghrib). Fasting teaches:

- Self-control
- Empathy for those less fortunate
- Patience

• Gratitude for Allah's blessings

The word "Ramadan" comes from the root word "ramida" or "ar-ramad," which means scorching heat or dryness – perhaps a reference to how fasting burns away sins!

HASSAN'S HONEST CHOICE

Hassan's pencil hovered over his math test, his heart pounding. The question seemed impossible – something about trains traveling at different speeds that made his head spin. From the corner of his eye, he could see Zain confidently filling in answers two rows ahead. Even Omar, still wearing a pair of ridiculous space-noise sneakers, appeared to be breezing through the test.

The numbers on Hassan's paper blurred as he remembered what was at stake. If he got an A on this test, it would bring his grade up enough to join the prestigious Math Club. His older sister Noor had been president of the Math Club three years ago, and everyone expected Hassan to follow in her footsteps.

Just then, Mrs. Parker stepped out to help another teacher with a technical issue. "I'll be back in two minutes," she announced. "Continue working quietly."

Hassan's eyes drifted to Yusuf's paper on the desk next to his. Yusuf was naturally gifted at math, and his answer sheet was clearly visible. All Hassan had to do was take one quick peek at that trains question...

The voice of Ustadh Kareem from yesterday's Islamic studies class echoed in his mind: "The Prophet Muhammad, peace be upon him, said that truthfulness leads to righteousness, and righteousness leads to Paradise. A person keeps speaking the truth until they are recorded as truthful with Allah."

Hassan gripped his pencil tighter. But this wasn't exactly lying, was it? He wasn't speaking any untruths. He just needed one small hint...

His inner debate was interrupted by a paper airplane that sailed across the room and landed perfectly on top of Karim's head. The class erupted in muffled giggles as Karim, who had been deep in calculation, jumped in surprise.

"Who threw that?" Karim whispered, trying to look stern but failing to hide his grin. Nobody confessed, though Hassan noticed Ibrahim, sat two rows behind Karim, suddenly becoming very interested in his eraser.

The brief distraction cleared Hassan's mind somewhat. He remembered the time last week when he'd helped old Mr. Wilson organize his tool shed. They had found an old broken watch, and Mr. Wilson had trusted Hassan to take it to the repair shop.

"I'm trusting you with this, son," Mr. Wilson had said. "It was my father's watch."

The way Mr. Wilson had trusted him with something so precious had made Hassan feel ten feet tall. That feeling of being trustworthy – wasn't it worth more than any grade?

Hassan took a deep breath and turned his paper slightly away from Yusuf's. He would rather fail honestly than pass through cheating. He started breaking down the trains problem step by step, the way Ahmad had taught him during their study sessions at the mosque library.

"First, identify what you know," he whispered to himself. "Then figure out what you need to find..."

Suddenly, the problem didn't seem quite so

impossible. By the time Mrs. Parker returned, Hassan had worked out an answer he felt confident about.

That afternoon, as Hassan walked home with his friends, Omar was still insisting that his light-up sneakers helped him think better during tests.

"They're scientifically proven to enhance brain power!" Omar declared, as his shoes made their signature *beep-whoosh* sound.

"Is that why you wrote that trains could travel at the speed of light?" Ibrahim teased.

"I was being creative!" Omar protested, making everyone laugh.

Hassan was quieter than usual, still thinking about the test. His friends noticed.

"Hey, you okay?" Karim asked. "That test was pretty tough."

"I... I had a chance to cheat," Hassan admitted. "But I didn't."

His friends fell silent, even Omar's shoes seeming to beep more softly.

"That must have been hard," Ahmad said thoughtfully. "But you know what? That's real success – not just getting the right answers, but getting them the right way."

When the graded tests were returned the next

week, Hassan's heart nearly stopped. There, at the top of his paper, was a big red B+. Not an A, but he had earned every point honestly.

"Good job, Hassan," Mrs. Parker said with a smile. "Your step-by-step solution to the trains problem was excellent. Have you considered joining Math Club? We could use problem-solving skills like yours."

Hassan blinked in surprise. "But... don't you need an A average?"

"We look for students who demonstrate strong mathematical thinking and integrity," Mrs. Parker explained. "Your detailed work shows both."

That evening, Hassan couldn't wait to tell his family the news. But when he got home, he found an unexpected visitor – Mr. Wilson, holding his repaired watch.

"The repair shop owner called me," Mr. Wilson said, his eyes twinkling. "Told me how my young friend insisted on paying for the repair from his own savings, even though it cost more than expected. Said he hadn't met such an honest young man in years."

Hassan's mother wiped a proud tear from her eye as he showed them his test. "SubhanAllah," she said. "Allah's blessings come in unexpected ways when we choose to be honest."

His father nodded. "There's a beautiful hadith where the Prophet Muhammad, peace be upon him, said: 'Guarantee me six things and I will guarantee you Paradise: tell the truth when you speak, keep your promises when you make them, when you are trusted with something fulfill your trust...'"

"I think I'm starting to understand that better now," Hassan said. "Being trustworthy isn't just about big things – it's about all the small choices too."

Later that night, as Hassan prepared for Isha prayer, he found a small package on his prayer mat. Inside was a handsome wristwatch with a note from Mr. Wilson: "For a young man who values truth more than convenience. Your honesty is worth more than any timepiece."

Hassan smiled, securing the watch on his wrist. The hands ticked steadily, like a gentle reminder that every moment brings a new choice to be truthful, to be trustworthy, to be the best version of yourself.

As he raised his hands to begin his prayer, Hassan felt at peace. He hadn't just passed a math test today – he had passed a more important test of character.

📖 *Islamic Knowledge Corner*

Did you know? Honesty (Sidq) and trustworthiness (Amanah) are fundamental values in Islam. The Prophet Muhammad (peace be upon him) was known as "Al-Amin" (The Trustworthy) and "As-Sadiq" (The Truthful) even before he received revelation.

The importance of honesty is emphasized in many verses of the Quran: "O you who believe! Be conscious of Allah, and be with those who are true (in word and deeds)." (9:119)

The Prophet Muhammad (peace be upon him) said: "Truthfulness leads to righteousness, and righteousness leads to Paradise. A person continues to tell the truth until they are written before Allah as truthful. Lying leads to wickedness, and wickedness leads to the Fire. A person continues to tell lies until they are written before Allah as a liar." (Sahih al-Bukhari)

Islamic teachings emphasize that true success comes not just from achieving goals, but from achieving them through permissible means while maintaining our integrity.

THE NEW KID'S PRAYER MAT

Yusuf clutched his backpack straps tightly as he stared up at Riverside Middle School. Everything about this new school felt different from his old one in the city – the sprawling sports fields, the small-town quiet, and most notably, the fact that he might be the only Muslim student here.

"Remember, Yusuf," his mother had said that morning while straightening his jacket, "being different isn't a weakness. It's an opportunity to share who you are."

Easy for her to say, Yusuf thought. She wasn't the one who had to figure out where to pray Dhuhr during lunch break.

His first few classes passed in a blur of new faces

and names. During history, a friendly boy named Michael invited him to sit at his lunch table. Things were going better than expected until Yusuf realized it was almost Dhuhr time.

"I need to go pray," he explained to Michael, pulling his rolled-up prayer mat from his backpack. "Do you know if there's a quiet room I could use?"

Michael looked confused but interested. "You pray during school?"

"Yeah, Muslims pray five times a day. One of them is during lunch hour."

"That's cool! You can use the empty study room near the library. I'll show you."

As they walked to the study room, Yusuf felt a mix of relief and nervousness. At his old school, there had been several Muslim students who prayed together. Here, he would be alone.

Or so he thought.

"Are you going to pray Dhuhr?" a voice asked as he entered the study room. A tall boy was arranging his own prayer mat in the corner. "I'm Waseem. I usually pray here during lunch."

Yusuf's face lit up. "Yes! I'm Yusuf. I just moved here."

As they prepared for prayer, more students peeked into the room curiously. Michael had apparently spread the word. Some watched respectfully, while others whispered among themselves.

The next day, Yusuf found a note taped to his locker: "Go back to where you came from!" His heart sank. He had hoped things would be different here.

During lunch, a group of older boys cornered him in the hallway near the study room.

"Hey, prayer boy!" one called out. "Why do you have to be so different? This is America!"

Yusuf's hands trembled, but he remembered his mother's words. Taking a deep breath, he turned to face them. "Would you like to learn why we pray?"

The boys seemed taken aback by his calm response.

"Actually, I would," said a new voice. It was Michael, stepping between Yusuf and the older boys. "And if Yusuf's different, then that makes our school better. Because now we can learn something new."

More students gathered around, including some who had watched him pray yesterday. To Yusuf's surprise, they seemed genuinely curious about his faith.

"Why do you pray five times a day?" "What's that mat for?" "How do you know which direction to face?"

Yusuf found himself explaining Islamic prayer to

an impromptu audience. He demonstrated how Muslims bow and prostrate, explained the significance of facing the Qibla, and shared how prayer helps him feel centered and peaceful throughout the day.

"It's like taking five daily breaks to remember what's really important," he explained. "It helps me be a better person."

The older boys who had tried to intimidate him drifted away, looking somewhat embarrassed. But others stayed, fascinated by this glimpse into a different way of life.

The next day, Yusuf found another note on his locker. His heart raced until he opened it: "Prayer room meeting at lunch. Bring extra mats!" It was signed by Michael and several other students.

When Yusuf arrived at the study room, he found not just Waseem, but also Michael and a group of students from different backgrounds. Some came to pray their own prayers, others to meditate, and some simply to support their new friend.

"We thought you shouldn't have to pray alone," Michael explained. "Plus, this room has the best quiet vibes in school."

As Yusuf laid out his prayer mat, he noticed something remarkable. The room that had once felt like a place to hide had transformed into a space of understanding and respect. Students would quietly enter during prayer times, some observing respectfully, others finding their own moment of peaceful reflection.

By month's end, the "Prayer and Meditation Room" (as it was now officially known) had become one of the most popular quiet spaces in school. The principal even installed arrow markers pointing toward Mecca, and put up a schedule showing prayer times alongside other faith traditions' meditation periods.

One afternoon, as Yusuf rolled up his prayer mat, he found a small package wrapped in blue paper. Inside was a beautiful new prayer mat with a card signed by his classmates: "Thank you for teaching us that being different makes us all better."

That evening, Yusuf's mother noticed him smiling as he prepared for Maghrib prayer.

"You were right, Mama," he said, carefully laying out his new prayer mat. "Being different isn't a weakness. It's a gift we can share with others."

As he began his prayer, Yusuf felt a deep sense of gratitude. His prayer mat had become more than just a place to pray – it had become a bridge between cultures, a teacher of understanding, and a reminder that sometimes the best way to overcome fear is to open our hearts to learning about each other.

Islamic Knowledge Corner

Did you know? The prayer mat (musalla or sajjadah in Arabic) is not actually required for prayer in Islam. Muslims can pray on any clean surface! However, prayer mats became traditional because:

• They provide a guaranteed clean space for prayer
  • They help create a dedicated space for worship
  • They protect the face during prostration
  • They help mark the direction of prayer (Qibla)

The five daily prayers are:

1 Fajr (dawn)

2 Dhuhr (noon)

3 Asr (afternoon)

4 Maghrib (sunset)

5 Isha (night)

These prayers serve as regular reminders to remember Allah and maintain spiritual consciousness throughout the day. The Quran says: "Indeed, prayer has been decreed upon the believers at specified times." (4:103)

GRANDFATHER'S GARDEN

I brahim stood at the edge of his grandfather's garden, or what was left of it. Where vibrant flowers and fruit trees had once bloomed, there were now only withered plants and dry soil. His grandfather – everyone in the neighborhood called him Dada Umar – had been in the hospital for three months, and his beloved garden had suffered in his absence.

"Everything can be brought back to life," Dada Umar said softly from his wheelchair, his eyes scanning the neglected garden. He had just returned home yesterday, and this was the first thing he had asked to see. "Allah shows us this miracle every spring, doesn't He?"

Ibrahim wasn't so sure. The garden looked pretty

dead to him. Even the apple tree where he used to do his homework was dropping brown leaves, even though it was only early summer.

"I don't know, Dada," Ibrahim sighed. "Maybe we should just clear everything out and start new?"

His grandfather's eyes twinkled. "Ah, but that would be like giving up on a friend just because they're going through a difficult time. Come here, let me tell you something."

Ibrahim wheeled his grandfather to the shade of the struggling apple tree. A few blessed moments passed with just the whisper of the wind through the dry leaves.

"Did you know," Dada Umar began, "that the Prophet Muhammad, peace be upon him, said that if someone has a sapling in their hand and the Day of Judgment begins, they should still plant it?"

Ibrahim looked at his grandfather in surprise. "But why? Wouldn't it be too late?"

"That's exactly the point, my dear grandson. It teaches us that doing good – like planting trees and caring for Allah's creation – is valuable in itself, regardless of whether we see the results." Dada Umar reached down and picked up a handful of dry soil, letting it sift through his fingers. "Every act of nurturing life is an act of worship."

Something stirred in Ibrahim's heart. He looked around the garden with new eyes, seeing not just what it was now, but what it could become again.

"Will you teach me how to bring it back, Dada?"

His grandfather's face lit up. "I thought you'd never ask! First, we need to understand what each plant needs. Gardens are like people – each one is unique and needs different kinds of care."

Over the next few weeks, Ibrahim spent every afternoon with his grandfather in the garden. They started small, with just one flower bed near the wheelchair ramp. Dada Umar taught him how to test the soil, when to water, and how to tell if a plant was salvageable.

"See these roots?" his grandfather showed him, gently lifting a withered plant. "They're still strong. Sometimes the strongest part of us is hidden underground."

Ibrahim learned that gardening required not just work, but patience and prayer. His grandfather would recite duas while they worked: "Allahumma aj'al fi qalbi nuran" (O Allah, place light in my heart) "Rabbi zidni 'ilma" (My Lord, increase me in knowledge)

"Why do you make dua while gardening?"

Ibrahim asked one day, carefully pruning a rose bush the way his grandfather had taught him.

"Because every growing thing glorifies Allah in its own way," Dada Umar explained. "When we help Allah's creation thrive, we join in their praise of Him."

Slowly but surely, the garden began to show signs of life. The rose bush sprouted new leaves. The apple tree's remaining leaves turned a healthier green. Even the soil seemed richer, darker.

Word spread through the neighborhood about the garden's revival. Children from the Islamic weekend school started dropping by to learn from Dada Umar. He taught them about companion planting – how certain plants help others grow better when planted together.

"Just like good friends," he would say with a smile. "We all help each other grow stronger."

One day, while Ibrahim was clearing weeds from around the vegetable patch, he found an old, rusted sign half-buried in the soil. After cleaning it off, he could read the faded words: "The Earth is a mosque."

"Ah, you found it!" his grandfather exclaimed. "I made that sign years ago to remind myself that everywhere we step is a place of worship. The Prophet Muhammad, peace be upon him, said the entire Earth was made a mosque for us. That means we have a responsibility to care for it."

As summer progressed, the garden transformed. The vegetable patch yielded its first tomatoes. Butterflies returned to the flower beds. Birds began visiting the apple tree again.

But the most beautiful transformation was in Dada Umar himself. With each plant that recovered, his eyes grew brighter. His physical therapy exercises became easier as he reached for plants and guided Ibrahim's hands in the soil.

One evening, as they sat in the garden after Maghrib prayer, watching the sunset paint the flowers in gold, Ibrahim noticed tears in his grandfather's eyes.

"Are you okay, Dada?"

"More than okay, my dear boy. I was worried, you know. Not just about the garden, but about passing on these teachings. Your generation has so many distractions – phones, games, social media. I feared the old ways of connecting with Allah through nature would be lost."

Ibrahim thought about this. "Maybe we can do both? I've been taking pictures of the garden's progress for my science project. And some kids from school want to start an environmental club based on what we've learned here."

His grandfather laughed with delight. "You see? The old and the new growing together, just like our garden!"

That weekend, the garden hosted its first community gathering since Dada Umar's return. Neighbors brought dishes to share, children played among the flowers, and Dada Umar held court under the apple tree, sharing gardening tips and wisdom with anyone who asked.

Ibrahim watched as his grandfather handed out seedlings he had carefully grown from cuttings. "Plant these with bismillah," he told each person, "and remember that you're not just growing plants – you're growing hope, beauty, and a closer connection to Allah."

Later that night, as Ibrahim helped his grandfather inside, they paused to look back at the garden in the moonlight.

"You know what the best part of gardening is?" Dada Umar asked.

"What?"

"It never ends. Each season brings new challenges and blessings. Just when you think you've learned everything, Allah shows you something new.

That's why it's such a perfect way to stay humble and keep learning."

Ibrahim nodded, understanding now why his grandfather loved this space so much. It wasn't just a garden – it was a living lesson in faith, patience, and the endless mercy of Allah.

"Dada," he said suddenly, "can we plant that sapling tomorrow? You know, the one you've been saving?"

"Even if it's the Day of Judgment?" his grandfather teased.

"Especially then," Ibrahim grinned. "Because doing good things is always worth it, right?"

Dada Umar smiled at Ibrahim. And once again the two of them looked out to the garden. Under the moonlight, it seemed to glow. Almost as if it was smiling back.

📚 *Islamic Knowledge Corner*

Did you know? Environmental conservation is strongly emphasized in Islamic teachings. The Quran and Hadith contain numerous references to the importance of protecting nature:

• The Quran describes nature as "ayat" (signs) of Allah, indicating that the natural world is a way to understand the Creator

- Muslims are encouraged to be "khalifah" (stewards) of the Earth
- The Prophet Muhammad (peace be upon him) established protected areas called "hima" for conservation
- He taught that planting trees is a form of ongoing charity (sadaqah jariyah)
- Islamic law includes specific provisions for water conservation and animal protection

The Prophet Muhammad (peace be upon him) said: "If any Muslim plants a tree or sows a field, and a human, bird or animal eats from it, it shall be reckoned as charity from him." (Sahih al-Bukhari)

This teaches us that environmental stewardship isn't just about conservation – it's a form of worship and a way to earn continuous rewards from Allah.

THE MIDNIGHT MOON SIGHTING

Zayn pressed his face against his bedroom window, squinting at the dark sky. Tomorrow might be Eid ul-Fitr – or it might not be. It all depended on whether anyone spotted the new crescent moon tonight.

"Zayn! Are you ready?" his father called from downstairs. "The mosque's moon-sighting committee is meeting in twenty minutes!"

"Coming, Baba!" Zayn grabbed his special backpack – the one he had spent all week preparing. Inside was everything a serious moon spotter might need: binoculars, a star chart, his notebook (for recording official observations), and most importantly, the telescope his parents had given him for his eleventh birthday.

This year, Zayn had been invited to join the moon-sighting committee as their "junior astronomer." He had earned this title after giving a presentation at the mosque about the lunar calendar, complete with a working model he'd built for the science fair.

The night air was crisp as Zayn and his father drove to Hilltop Park, where the committee always gathered for moon sighting. The park offered a perfect view of the western horizon, away from the city's bright lights.

"Do you think we'll see it tonight, Baba?" Zayn asked, clutching his telescope case.

"Allah knows best," his father replied. "That's why we look with our eyes rather than just relying on calculations. It reminds us that some things can't be perfectly predicted – they require patience and faith."

When they arrived, several families were already setting up their viewing equipment. Children ran around with glow sticks while adults consulted charts and adjusted telescopes. The atmosphere was festive – after all, they might be among the first to spot the moon that would end Ramadan.

Sheikh Abdul, the head of the moon-sighting committee, waved Zayn over. "Ah, here's our young astronomer! Come, help me set up the main telescope."

As Zayn carefully helped assemble the large telescope, Sheikh Abdul explained the importance of their task. "You know, this tradition goes back to the time of the Prophet Muhammad, peace be upon him. He told us to begin and end Ramadan based on sighting the crescent moon. Today, we continue this practice, connecting us to Muslims across time and space."

The sun had set, but they needed to wait for the sky to darken enough to spot the thin crescent. Zayn used this time to share his moon facts with anyone who would listen.

"Did you know," he told a group of younger children, "that the Arabic word for moon is 'qamar,' but the new crescent is called 'hilal'? And the moon doesn't actually emit light – it reflects the sun's light!"

"But why does it change shape?" a small girl asked.

"Well," Zayn began, pulling out his notebook where he'd drawn diagrams, "it's all about how the moon orbits Earth..."

Suddenly, someone shouted from the other side of the hill. "Look! Over there!"

Everyone rushed to their telescopes and binoculars. Zayn's hands trembled with excitement as he adjusted his telescope, scanning the horizon where others were pointing.

"I see something!" he called out. "But... I think it's an airplane."

Sheikh Abdul patted his shoulder. "Good observation, Zayn. It's important to be accurate and honest in moon sighting. Better to say 'I'm not sure' than to make a mistake."

The minutes ticked by. Some families spread blankets and shared snacks. Others told stories about moon sightings from years past. The younger children played "lunar tag," chasing each other with their glow sticks creating crescent shapes in the dark.

Just when some people were beginning to pack up, Zayn noticed something through his telescope – a tiny sliver of silver against the darkening sky.

"Sheikh Abdul!" he whispered, trying to keep his voice steady. "Could you please check this position?"

The Sheikh looked through Zayn's telescope, then quickly moved to the larger one. A crowd gathered, holding their breath.

"Allahu Akbar!" Sheikh Abdul finally announced. "The hilal has been sighted!"

The park erupted in celebration. "Eid Mubarak!" people called out, hugging each other. Parents pulled out hidden bags of candy, and children squealed with delight.

Zayn's father hugged him tight. "MashaAllah, my son. You were the first to spot it!"

But Zayn was already busy drawing the moon's exact position in his notebook and recording the time. "As the junior astronomer," he explained seriously, "I have to document everything properly."

Sheikh Abdul smiled. "Indeed you do. And tomorrow, you can help me announce it to the community."

That night, as messages about the moon sighting spread through phone calls and texts, Zayn lay in bed thinking about how a tiny sliver of moon could bring so much joy to so many people. His father had been right – some things were more special because they couldn't be perfectly predicted.

The next morning, Zayn woke up early, too excited to sleep. As he helped his mother prepare Eid breakfast, he could hear the takbir being called from the mosque: "Allahu Akbar, Allahu Akbar, La ilaha illa Allah..."

His special notebook lay open on the kitchen counter, displaying his careful drawings of the crescent moon. Next to them, he had written: "Date: Last night of Ramadan Time: 9:17 PM Location: Hilltop Park Observer: Zayn Abdullah Official Status: Junior Astronomer Notes: The new moon was spotted! Eid tomorrow, inshaAllah!"

And below that, in his best handwriting: "Ya Allah, thank you for letting me be part of this beautiful tradition. Please let me see many more new moons with my community. Ameen."

📚 *Islamic Knowledge Corner*

Did you know? The Islamic calendar is lunar, meaning it follows the phases of the moon. Each month begins with the sighting of the new crescent moon (hilal). This is why:

- Islamic months can be 29 or 30 days long
- The same Islamic date falls on different days of the solar calendar each year
- Ramadan and other Islamic celebrations move through the seasons over the years

The Prophet Muhammad (peace be upon him) said: "Fast when you see it (the new moon) and break your fast when you see it." This tradition of moon sighting:

- Unites communities in a shared experience

- Teaches patience and reliance on Allah
- Connects Muslims to the natural world
- Reminds us that Allah's signs are all around us

The Quran mentions the phases of the moon as one of Allah's signs: "And the moon, We have measured for it phases until it returns like an old date stalk. The sun is not permitted to overtake the moon, nor does the night outstrip the day, but each, in an orbit, is swimming." (36:39-40)

www.ingramcontent.com/pod-product-compliance
Lightning Source LLC
La Vergne TN
LVHW041237080426
835508LV00011B/1248